THE ROLLER COASTER BEGINS

BOOK 1

THOMAS BURSON

This is a work of fiction. All of the characters, names, incidents, organizations, and dialogue in this novel are either the products of the author's imagination or are used fictitiously.

Archway Publishing books may be ordered through booksellers or by contacting:

Archway Publishing
1663 Liberty Drive
Bloomington, IN 47403
www.archwaypublishing.com
844-669-3957

ISBN: 978-1-6657-5716-4 (sc)
ISBN: 978-1-6657-5717-1 (e)

Library of Congress Control Number: 2024903666

Print information available on the last page.

Archway Publishing rev. date: 02/27/2024

CONTENTS

Preface viii

Fallow 1
Art 2
A beach Comber's Lament 4
Backwards is easy with so much to unlearn 6
First dandelion Afternoon 8
Sanguine & Sagacious 10
Sandbox Pirates 11
Crockery, Shards, and Archaeology 13
Sundials 14
Sand In the Shoe 16
One Stone Turned 17
Should Reason Deny 19
Half Finished 20
Grave Etching 22
The End of Concordance 24
Times Of Day 25
In My Time of Shadows 27
Late Night Storms Interrupt TV 29
The Mistress and Her Mate 30
Reflections in An Antique Mirror 31
The Shoot Must First Break The Earth 33
Maybe There's more. 35
The End of a Drunk 36
Moon Wine 38
Moon madness 39
Birds like eyebrows wink at me 40
You didn't steal my heart I gave it to you 42
Nation Builders 44
Some days you know you are different 46
Sorcery in Training 48

She Is . . . 50
Catching Up 51
Postmortem of a Suicide 53
Chocolate and Tangerine 54
Before We Spoke Of Love 55
Curse Maintenance 56
Tweener 58
Counseling 59
Confessions of an Ancient with Suicidal Tendencies 62
Cause There Is Poetry 64
Not Too Long, But Long Enough 65
Adam Discovers Eden, Too 67
It was only yesterday . . 68
First Lesson 70
Take the Pot Down, Please 71
Crewel Points 73
Warrior Chiefs 75
Self-Taught 77
Atlas Tries To Understand Metaphysics 79
Snow 81
Hylas 82
A Rake 84
The Hunt 85
Promise 87
The world was cast adrift 88
Penny Wise, Dollar Short 90
How To Speak Many Languages 91
Trees Are Thunder In The Fog 92
Learning to Choose 93
To Emily: As Only I Knew Her 94
Cranes & Kites 96
Grammar 97
Raising Sand Dollars 99
Growing Pinions 101
Carpenter 103

Another Day at 5825 105
My Teacher 106
Neighborwood 108
Migration of the Heart 110
Berries for Breakfast 112
Nor'easter: The Storm's A-commin' 113
a stranger 114
A Word to the Wise 115
Symbiotic 117
Can You Hear the Ice Cry Against Spring's Arrival? 119
Dementia 121

Bibliography 123

PREFACE

I started writing at sixteen, because of a poem "Message" by Allen Ginsberg. I wrote every night where I went to boarding school. It was a Quaker school my family had gone to since its beginning in 1799. When it was considered co-ed because girls and boys were taught in the same building, the only time they saw each other was at evening meals and on Sundays when they sat in separate sections of the Meeting House. The exception was that after Meeting brothers and sisters and first cousins were allowed to gather at the center of the building under the watchful eye of the teacher on duty. There they would pass books for spiritual enlightenment to each other. These books were hollowed out and had notes folded up in them to members of the opposite sex. There were called K.O.B.'s which stood for Kindness of Bearer. Romances were carried on this way that proved so vibrant and strong that members of the student body later married upon matriculation. When I went there starting in 1964, they had just made it okay for students of the opposite sex to meet in classrooms after dinner without a chaperon. K.O.B.'s were still written and carried to the center building and traded after study hall. This was at 9:30 PM. It was a matter of pride to show off how many you'd received until you were a junior when such things seemed trivial. I wrote love poetry to one girl after another, sometimes several on a given evening. I probably should of been as dedicated in doing my studies, but such is youth. I found out when I returned for my fifth year Alumni Day that when a woman on the dorm received one of my K.O.B's they read it aloud to all the other woman on dorm. If I had known that I probably would not of written another. I have since had a few woman ask me if I wanted the ones I had written returned. I would tell them all, I had kept copies. I did. I still have each of them. I don't know why, most aren't worth reading. We all have to begin somewhere.

I now am seventy-three. I am grateful to the people I have known who have supported me in my efforts and challenges in writing poetry for the last fifty-five years since my high school graduation. I think I have gotten a little better. I read them at a little coffee shop in Manassas, VA called Jirani's. It is a once a month reading run by a group called Spilled Ink. These people and an online group called All Poetry are owed a great deal of thanks for their support, their criticisms and insights. Without them I would have never reached a point where I would be publishing this book. We are only as healthy as the friends we participate with. Fortunately, I have been surrounded by human beings who support me to be far more than I would ever recognize myself to be.

FALLOW

These angels of grace
come silently into the shadows
where our fears hide. The ache
left after scabs scar is kissed
quietly by their patient tears.

When we rail at God and damn
the abusers who sit proud
in this kingdom of chaos,
they kneel quietly before us
sifting the winds for gifts.
Even if we cannot see the value
of these invisible seeds,
they hold them, patiently waiting for us.

Understanding is too often cursed
For all we see is the rack and ruin
of dreams crashed upon some
uncaring circumstance. God
never gives us results, only
these angels who will guide us
in the planting and strengthen us
so we may fully harvest.

Calloused knees in prayer
need to be bent to the furrows.

6:37 PM
04-06-16
Stafford, VA

ART

Truth is a revelation,
we experience. Each indelible
produces change
validation.
Until then, we are argument
relative to cause and effect
declaring the truth lies in outcomes.

Who we are is not married to pretense.
When the clothes don't fit,
No amount of pretend will produce splendor.
Our disbelief in our own magnificence
doesn't allow us to do more than quiver
in our shadows unaware of the light we cast.

How often when we start to uncurl
discover how to straighten our spine
have we faltered in the face of strength,
backed away from the possibility we can be?

The lie is found in our disbelief,
our lack of faith in the greatest of beings.
When we let go yesterday and learn today
is not a replication of the past, but discover
what is born out of it. We might see

potential is a ghost built to frighten the weak.
Being is a foundation not an end.
Each moment allows for invention.
Creation is not the lie. For we are born
to bring things together and to mold
from the substance about us what we are.

2211
01-31-16
Stafford, VA

A Beach Comber's Lament

I swallow the sounds
oceans run out, sink into the sand;
gulls cry out, follow the sacred helix,
plunge the water's face, flap in haste,
pull up, strut on the shore, argue
over the leavings of tourists, like gypsies.

The anniversary is days away.
Summer's floods has started:
sandcastles half-eroded, beach umbrellas
blossomed, screams of children woven
'round gulls, parents eyeing strange
clouds for rain, and every shop
ready to swallow any passerby.

The sun sinks into the horizon beyond the marsh,
the heron flows head and beak beneath wing.

I cannot hear your footsteps on the sand beside me.
I see bright colors in a store window
find myself tightening, then realizing
your hand will not pull at me to look, just to see.
Feel the tide of ghosts. Memories rise wash and sink.

You never stop living inside of me.

The moon is full
tide high.

I have gotten too old to start again.
I hear a ship's horn and it is too dark

I am too far away to know where it is coming from
or where it is going to. I can feel the breeze start up,
taste the salt in the air and I have not a care.
Someday — may I never expect it —
I will sink into the sea and let you take me away.

1328
05-28-12
IAD

BACKWARDS IS EASY WITH SO MUCH TO UNLEARN

I can tell you being brave ain't enough
I wish I knew ahead of time how it would
all turn out. Then, I could act without a doubt.
But, baby, I feel I am just not brave enough for love.

Imagine if you will there was a magic spell.
One, where you started at the end, as I will tell.
We already had all the kids and I was gray;
you were starting to wrinkle just a bit.
We curled against each other when we went to bed.
We finished each other's sentences, cause
we knew what was going to be said.

We watch all the graduations
helped heal all their scars. Taught the girls
boys aren't any better and don't let 'em get too far.
Helped our sons be gentle and know it is
the best way to display strength, 'nuff said.
We felt safe in what we were doing because like I said,
we had already seen them when they were wed.

Living life backwards makes love a cake walk,
trust comes easy 'cause it's already been taught.
I don't have to be brave cause the truth is known,
you are only one who makes me house a home.

We can laugh about it as we move back to the time,
when I knocked on your door half out of my mind,
asked as quickly as I could if you would go to the prom.
Saw your mom over your shoulder smile and wink,
while you looked at me and said you had to think.
I don't know what I'd do if I didn't already know
it is more than okay to be in love and go slow.

The only funny part of this regressive scene
is when I lived in another state and didn't know
you or what was going to be my fate. But you can relate
seeing as you were a little girl with golden curls
who didn't yet know the man who would be her world.

Yes, living backwards makes life a cake walk.
Trust comes easy cause it's already been taught.
Heartbreak heals quickly cause you know what you sought
has already been found and will never be lost.

1833
03-12-2020
Stafford, VA

FIRST DANDELION AFTERNOON

We were on a hillside of our romance.
Caught in the straw chewing philosophies
that drew deep arguments about the shapes
formed by clouds. Knew the gods demand
the proper interpretations of secrets sent
draped across the landscapes of the heavens.

I had chased walked talked you
out of a cloistered tomb of winter demands
where the heat smothered pushed you
into pillows wall paper and the constant racket
TV fills a silence with limitless promise undelivered.

First Spring days are sacred.

Wishes, sent to the clouds by elfin winds
draped on the back of dandelion ballerinas,
become secrets released on the cusp
a warm day's passion freed
in a flutter of flight quail flushed.

We fell onto our backs after rock dancing
'cross the stream dividing the valley.
Masters of the world — a quilt spread before us.
You decreed that work should cease,
Maypoles woven in an early March,
brownies invited to attend in crocus bonnets.
The twinkle in your eyes as you pushed
your hands into the pockets of low slung jeans.

Summer could not leap into my arms enough

We held hands as we drew images from the cloud's display
felt brave as we trembled with the rising fog of desire.
Rose to our feet tossed dandelions aside and raced
across the fields as if we could out distance
the first signs of love awoken before we knew what it meant.

1154
12-30-2020
22556

SANGUINE & SAGACIOUS

We were the wind, the white sails
feeling the hand thrum of the waves against the hull.
Your hands the tiller, the path from the dawn.
I, the breath that spreads the sails, the outlook for shoals.

Harbored, the last early light draining pink
across the horizon. Sails reefed. Our backs
sharing a spine as we sipped beer
felt the hands of each other's breath.

My pinions read the wind, I watch the shadows move in the sea.

We feasted outside in the final crepuscular blush,

feeding each other saucy tidbits, kissing the marinara
away from lips and chins. Suck the oyster's from the shell,
fingers slippery with desire, trace lips, light fires.

I watched the moon's shadows walk with creamy hands
across your tawny back and into your storied tresses.
Surfacing from your oracular dreams — seeress, my Aphrodite —
you led me in a dance on the tops of the white crested waves.

Heroes of Illiad, followers of Odysseus — we are swans on black waters.

0013
10-30-07
Alexandria HD, VA

SANDBOX PIRATES

Memories tie themselves
round tree trunks, door knobs —
weave particulars into song —
catch your heart
with the right twist of shadow.

We never forget when we have been touched.

I live with ghosts.
Tales children create —
memories, kite tails, in blue skies —
when friends and I were wild eyed,
pledged to a brotherhood full
of unconquerable dreams.

Families move, dreams
lost in packing creates.
Promises forged on playgrounds
forgotten like stone
markers for hopscotch.

Except, when I creep through the rock
deep in my foundation, find relics
holding hot afternoon catch,
tackle football on front yard grass,
all my futures buried in my past.

Friends lost to twist of time and parent's
course in job demands. But, I understand
we made ourselves believe we could be
anything our imagination perceived.
Now, I am nothing like I could foresee
but so much more for the practice I got
with friends riding waves in a sandbox sea.

2357
03-03-09
Washington, DC

CROCKERY, SHARDS, AND ARCHAEOLOGY

Old men melt into clay.
Their stories left for children,
get into the flesh. Our shadow selves
confuse us with their reality,
when we crumble into dust.

Porcelain, ceramics, all the jewelry
of the earth, holds us, speaks silently,
becomes more important than the meal.
Wisdom is an art form, far greater than the words.

Hearts are used to temper the steel of swords.

The times change like tides. History
is used to explain the flotsam left.
We find patterns, to create cause,
in randomness. We are always surprised
when we find our elders actually had rich lives.

In my past life, I was a proud dirt farmer.
Peat roof, mud floor — potatoes for dinner —
gruel with bits of mill stones for breakfast.
Everyone, I know, had royalty in their past
knows the language of ermine. I only know callus.

Dreams slip from the wings of migratory birds, snowy petals.

2204
11-21-07
Alexandria, VA

SUNDIALS

Telling time by shadows
sundials on the green
tall trees holding on to secrets
as they sweep away the dawn
keeping the coolness and comfort
when summer's sun comes along.

How the day unfolds,
the pattern of creases traced
new visions of possibilities created
out of where we have been
tangled with the view of where
we will be.

Morning joys employed are best
when shared with someone who
at more than a glance understands
the laughter found in a dance.

Watch the squirrels play.
The dash the dart
sudden start
sudden stop
race 'round tree
tumbled through grasses play feels so free.

The day goes by
shadows thicken
collect in hollows
bring back the secrets
told between burrow and fir
whispers of leaf and wren
evening songs of once begins again.

She comes out to the hammock swing
her soft voice a song I love to hear sing.
We gather the fruits of labor's cost
we share the joys, sorrows, and maybes
each day has to mend.
Shake out our efforts
return to home
shut the door
a day well spent.

1019
06-07-19
22556

SAND IN THE SHOE

Art provokes

It does not answer.

There are doors, a plenty.
We open them, one by one;
most are banal, a few personally embarrassing.
We feel we have wasted our time.

The artist is more than, simply, an entertainer.
We are lured into rooms, stirred with emotions
we often never knew; gifted with meaning
leaves us richer than any simple truth provides.

Art can give us a life we cannot put down.

The greatest art?
what we create for ourselves.

1316
01-23-13
Porter Library, VA

ONE STONE TURNED

Come,
walk with me a while.
Let us delve into a moment
find each other
before the conversation begins.

These rocks skipping across the water
collecting on the lake bottom.

Life flashes by
too often like watching landscapes
from a train. The car empty
no matter how we laugh, act
no one is there to notice.
We wave to:
the farmer on the tractor,
the car at the crossing,
the travelers on the plane.

The train seems to be an express.

As much as I hate the trip
I do not want it to end.

If I landed on top of you after being tossed
by some small child so they could laugh
count the skips and turn to a friend
proudly share the number and say, “There.”

If I landed, would you let me stay?

1239
08-05-17
22556

SHOULD REASON DENY

We are, often, too ready to deny
when called to let our wonder take flight.
The stars of a good night filling a sky with light
until the oceans of possibility outweigh our senses.

She — is there not always a partner,
the first part of love — us — and greater than you or me —
came into my life in the crescendoes of thunder
followed by the sudden plunging rush of rain
pounding a roof, until it feels as if all is to be
a crumble beneath a Lord's pestle. She awoke
the first bridging signs of a rainbow.

I could do nothing less than follow. The crescendo
that waves of magic create is all too often missed.
We let doubt fashion a pretense of wisdom and leave
ourselves hollowed by our denials. I prayed
I was not so foolish and let my footprints
dance along the shore of her delights.

As the sun shredded the twilight with a final burst of light,
I wove myself into the breeze, caught the final joy
tossed on the highlights of life in the trees
and let myself roll into the final echoes of her laughter
before the night stole my chances to follow her home.

1841
08-10-19
2255

HALF FINISHED

It was time to move.

The walls were crushed with books.
No way all of them could go. No way I could
part with any of them. I opened a book of poems,
Neruda and his "101 Love poems."

The dust was thick. I remember when I read it so often it
became dog eared, torn and looked like a refugee.
Inspiration is a conversation and I am always searching
for a partner. This was ice of the friends who carried me
lit fires in kindling when I thought was a desert.

I opened the cover, the title page half torn
and then the note fell out. She must have left it there
expecting me to find it. When the door closed
I left it on the shelf and somehow they were as one.

I slipped it in my pocket, tossed the book into the keep pile.
It was late, time to eat. I hit the light and left the room.
Days went by and laundry got piled high. I was at the washer
checking pockets and the note fell out.

Forgot where it came from. Opened it.

"you are the spring whose water I never can drink enough.
you refresh me and chill me and leave me wishing for more.
You are more than I can hold and sometimes a storm, I fear."

Sunsets, so ordinary, breath stealing
she walked out the door, hands up in the air
I didn't understand. I thought it meant it was over
she couldn't tell me and I didn't believe enough

I didn't know how
to trust what is real.

2144
03-13-19
22556

GRAVE ETCHING

i.

So much of life goes un-lived.

It is almost as if
we need illness
so we can recognize health.

or

is it
we are
so unhealthy
we look at health
as an alien intrusion.

ii.

Well seasoned, winter
unyielding, roots: permafrost
even as spring sings to our heart
and summer heats to curdling
dreams we once planned on acquiring.

We are creators in our soul of souls.
What we have made, brought into being
becomes our anchors to living, sense
the need, each day's quota of importance.

iii.

Tell the young two things:

Life runs quickly through your fingers,
live it deeply and savor all its flavors.

It is not what you acquire that you will
measure yourself by, toys come and go.
It will be the things you have created,
filled with your sense of self, you will
measure yourself against their worth.

iiii.

As you begin to count sunsets,
their diminishing numbers —
may the dawns bring smiles
leave each day richer

2331
04-09-16
22556

THE END OF CONCORDANCE

Sharp, cold the off shore rain
complains of aches and how the wind
has stolen it from the sea. It penetrates
my clothes, raises bumps on my skin, steals
what little warmth hides in my hands.

I can smell the waves long before
I can hear them, feel the way they fall
before I see their froth's course fill
the horizon. I always knew your shadow,
the after shave's sharp sting on the face, your heat
strong shoulder's absorbing my tears.

Salt bites the tongue, sharpens
the savor of flavors. Brine preserves
transforms. I taste it in every streak
you kissed from my dirty face.

I can remember. Memories have their own flame.
It gutters and dies when the floors creak.
I turn my head to where I would find your smile.
Then, I know, even the house remembers how you
moved. Anger mixes with pain, my shoulders sag
under the weight of the memory of hands.

1356
11-09-07
Alexandria H.D., VA

TIMES OF DAY

I.

I heard you before
your shadow laid its head
upon my heart: a wind held
its breath. The first light broke
the silence, I heard
exhaled, a breeze. The starlings clattered out of the trees,
a rush of busy hot with gossip.

II.

Before we, apes, placed our feet
upon the hard ground, stopped roaming
branches — we must have dreamed
flight would come. We would be leaved
with feathers, a kaleidoscope of colors.
We would
swirl around each other above tree tops
haunting lifetimes — the moment we were birds.

III.

When darkness was a taste, your eyes
were afire and my tongue was raw.

The moon danced on the froth. You stood
on the crest of the dune, the wind

holding onto your clothes.
You looked as if you could

step off into the sky
stroll amongst the stars

savor the flavors
eternity tied in your hair.

IV.

When the house is
empty,
I sit
in the garden
hear you in the wind
find you
blossoms erupt

1932
11-15-11
IAD

IN MY TIME OF SHADOWS

When I weep, let it not be
for me alone. Let there be strength
to confront disappointment with dignity,
loss with ingenuity, and death . . .
let death be faced unselfishly.

The passing of a loved one, after the shattering,
allows me to recognize how deeply I was gifted.
In the moment of tears, let this pain
be shadowed by all the richness
they shared with me in living.

Let not my enemies see victory
in my pain. For I would be strong
enough for them to know their slight
their negative behaviors are beneath
my dignity to recognize. It is
not pride, for all that I have pride enough,
it is in an effort to be humble
allow God to be in charge of judgment.
I do my best when I do not let myself
be encumbered by their judgments.

For all my efforts to behave
with integrity and rise
ready for the promise of each day —
I readily acknowledge how imperfect
I am. How quickly I become petty
at the hurt of a sight, fall into
the dance of one-upmanship
when I would prove myself worthy.

So please, help me be refreshed of spirit,
Lord. Help me see the Light, you bring
to every human heart. Help me focus
upon it and join with the Light — so we
can dance in its brightness share the joy
love brings and be refreshed by sharing.

Amen

1248
06-29-15
22556

LATE NIGHT STORMS INTERRUPT TV

It was where the branching began
the fractals still in primary, sense
still blandished as if it could provide
explanation. Gods answer for many things.
The rest are held as divine mystery.
Ships at sea can only face the oncoming wave
leave meaning for wiser practitioners
who know the art of sailing is more than a star
less than luck and all the heart you bring to it.

Storms are only nonsense and noise
to those who do not need to survive them.

There are those who claim to know
as if they have access to a book of answers.
We send our children to school. They learn
to make sure they have the right answer.
Wisdom is a light those who manage
the pretense of intelligence claim to know.
They still shiver in the snow when they have
Forgotten to prepare properly. Blame and guilt —
noise tossed around to avoid being responsible.

We now are not superstitious but follow the dictates
of logic ignoring all anomalies to the contrary.

So often we claim to be able to make sense
out of what is going on before someone pulls the plug.

2059
06-12-13
22556

THE MISTRESS AND HER MATE

She was the shimmer of the first cast
the wave racing across the shore, foam
dancing with the white wine of moonlight.

He — then shaped and carved craft, the art
found in the apprenticed mystery, where men
gather tales of their coming of age
spin them into the yearning shapes of the crafted art —

he heard her as he sliced the waters, feeling
the sleek parting like silk cloth to a tailor's art.
The parabolas of Flying Fish in the elongated leaps
heralds to her gifts as the birds soared, cried
and crashed into her body lifting back up
the prizes from kisses caught in their beaks.

The waves, the fury, the long sleek calm stretching
from horizon to horizon in an eternal arc of desire,
he danced for her whims and mastered her charms
taking what he needed going where he wanted
yet, never leaving, never saying goodbye

never going to the empty hourglass in the middle
of continental rest, with only the sun to love
in burning fury. NO

he slept upon her rocking breast, felt her kisses
in the moist breath of a morning breeze and forever
sang to the stars at night with the chorus of whales
stretching his paean of love to touch the first
morning star waking upon the horizon.

2154/ 06-30-11/ Alexandria, VA

Reflections in an Antique Mirror

Aphorisms are tidy.
My life tends to sprawl
while attempting to maintain
an air of dignity
amidst disheveled heaps of paper
stained bed sheets and lopsided rainbows.

Always

ready to encourage
anybody
who is going to climb
whatever holy of holies beckons.
Set to prime a sense of togetherness
among refugees and their hearts of hope —
I know, soon enough, I will recognize the subtle hints,
my job is done, my ready smile no longer needed.
They are uncomfortable.
I do not belong; I should not hang around
so long.

One rainy night
away
from a shadow
a half turn into the back alley, forever,
I leave full moons to wolves
crowns to the egos that would be king.
I am happy,
just, to sing,
whatever, the newest tune of blues
will do
go bring another princess
into my life
to complain about the pea.

1601
09-19-16
Kent Island, MD

THE SHOOT MUST FIRST BREAK THE EARTH

Out of the grunt, the groan, the howl
when the moon rose too large in a star-filled sea
comes the language where I separate the you
from me.

Fire sparks blown to flame, both light and night
are never the same. The ghosts of memories come
spin their web from gossamer threads of wind.
Language: some call a shaman's gift, the code of seers
and poets.

Ride the mountain tops like steeds of glory, sit against
the ice and snowy blasts and in the gray land, where fog
whispers on the surface of the marsh, one learns
the land, talks to itself, moves from lake to reed
to rain.

Silence is where the lips of God allow us to hear what
we cannot speak. Revelation to grow until the tsunami
rock the soul with rebirth and wings. Perfection is not man's.
The music of lapping waters heralds footprints and a hand
reaching to a heart.

Art began as planets coalesced. Recognition began
with the waking of intelligence. Creation demands creators.
Only the humble can move the clay to a shape that holds
another's breath. No matter how much we may prance and crow,
it is only the hollow beating on the chest to hide how
unsure we are of our vision in the hands of others.

Reverence is a place we come to. Silence evoked
is the greatest testimony of the awe we hold. The blank page:
a beginning where our imagination quivers with all to be.

2157
12-11-16
Stafford, VA

MAYBE THERE'S MORE. . .

Most mistook it for roots,
the way the knuckles came
up through the soil, the trunk
rough bark and the eye lost
it quickly in the morning mist.
They hadn't felt the house shake,
Jake understood, some people
most people are never to know.

He felt the breeze wind its way.
Knew it wasn't a summer frolic.
Listened to it shift, a long breath.

Magic must be protected.
Those that don't believe destroy
it in the process of trying
to prove the negative.
They always achieve their beliefs.

It left before the rains cleared the mist.
Most didn't realize anything had changed,
a few shook their heads and figured
they had been imagining things.

Jake's luck changed, but he wasn't telling.
Wisdom grows slowly.

1257
07-23-17
Stafford, VA

THE END OF A DRUNK

i.

He tells you he is a disabled veteran:
claim to his hope of respect. His skin icteritious
arms weak, belly distended. He claims
it's only a little weight. You listen with
a jaundiced ear as he reaches for the bottle
a little nip, just to ease the pain.

ii.

He sits up all night, TV night light.
sips a little off the ice now and then.
As the sun crawls under the curtains
yellow and amber, he blinks
puts his arms behind his head.
passes out.

iii.

He sees things now. Baby bobcats around
the fish pond, their pointed ears yellow
eyes. Liver, a sharp pain, he uses the
walker to ease the hurt when he must get
to the bathroom and miss the toilet.
A world washed out, he asks his sister if
she has seen the child with tattoos
hiding under the blanket on the couch.

iv.

He stands by the window, curtains open.
Leans on the cane, glass in the other hand.
Tells me, he doesn't get out like he used to.
He used to be bronze, a warrior.

He wears long sleeves and long johns without
change for weeks. He is always freezing.

v.

Onyx
without stars
he coughs, spits in the basket
reaches for a cigarette, but can't find the light.
Leans back, hands behind head.
waits
silent for the beginning of a film

12:08 PM
3/28/13
Stafford, VA

Moon Wine

A rivulet of moonlight leaked
through the window catching a cheekbone
a silver stone danced by the stream, glancing
off the buttons of your blouse making each a pebble
to be caught in the hand. Then, the sands parted before
stone slipped away to fall in silken magic across the bed.

My fingers, quicksilver sliding from the bud of lips
rise of chin, down the sluiceway of the neck, I rode
the white water foam of moonlight between the rising
swell across the flutter of belly -- the rich flesh of promise
the rising flash of rapids danced in Erato's music
as Selene played with our senses until laughter poured
through the white waters and our hands clutched
each others belts for safety as we leaned back.
Spinning around our moonlight spot,
dancing, dancing till we stood still
the universe smeared around us. Glowing with the pale
moon's fires, we tumbled to the ground, a puddle —
otter madness on a slippery bank. Tugging at our roots.

The bark of Levi's shredded in joy as we gleefully gamboled
over flesh twined with a magical moon of plaited delights.
The cave of shadows drew us together as gyrations and celebrations
cascaded across covers and we breathed flesh and bone-filled
hot madness scattered 'round passion's feathered flight.

MOON MADNESS

Your finger silenced my lips. Your eyes, moon full of light,
brought kisses that rained upon my shores till I was drenched
muddy and molded to your form. The wild weave of you
threaded around in silver twine caught the last splash of moonlight
cast open the hollow darkness of the vanishing stream along
your legs. My hands divined the mystery of energy from toe to thigh
listened to the wind suddenly cry from the tree tops. The elastic
stretched out into the moment and the veil fell from the shrine.
We knew we were leaving footprints in granite.

Volcanoes rise out of the crash and grind of continental plates
give curve and fold to earth as mountains climb towards stars

We watched each other's hands -- moths attracted to the light —
swirl on the new earth. Revelations of promise, born again
in the caverns of each chambered heart, rubies caught growing.
Tender, we are the ancient young, full of the knowledge.
Our past shed, we kissed the whorls of our identities, traced
the masks of our faces, felt the waters that rose out of us.
We let our breath blow the embers of moonlight
into fires. We forged tomorrows that eternity could not erode.

The moon set during the burning.
No night was ever again the same.

8:22 PM
1/11/08
Alexandria, VA

BIRDS LIKE EYEBROWS WINK AT ME

Morning eases her eyes open
brings the focus of edges
against a fog burning away
turned into wispy ghosts by a hungry wind.
The outdoors breathes light
through the windows, quiet household sentinels.
The potter's hands mutter in clay
before the wheel starts, decisions
to be made, visions clarified.
The woodcarver strokes his tools
remembers where he stopped, wants
the grain of wood to awaken his fingerprints;
see to the center of his heart
what emerges in the flesh of the wood.
Before the day steals the maybe away
artists feel possibilities rain.
Craftsmen find the path their creations must
follow no matter what temptations hide in dreams.
Giving birth is a journey forgotten at the bearing.
Labor brings its own fruit. Each plucked
savored and used on the relentless march to the day's end.

The cacophony of beginnings slips
from aches and moans, hesitations resolve,
noise finds synchronicity and the music finds its voice —
begins — sways with a woman's hips,
finds its drumbeat in the hearts and passions
our artists bring to imbue their creations with
a fire that leaves us with a hushed awe.
Morning slips away unnoticed.
The world shakes away the last blankets of darkness.
The potter breathes a glow of remembered hips
the fullness of the urn flourishes beneath his fingers.
The wood shavings are swept away tracing
swirls from the bench to the floor.
The carver sharpens his tools and hones an edge that waits
to taste his dream as it is revealed in the wood.
Days are always accentuated by their beginnings
given breath by the wands of light's magical appearance.

3:42 PM
10-15-11
IAD

YOU DIDN'T STEAL MY HEART I GAVE IT TO YOU

The waves approach, gulls —
swirling helix, wind —
a wrap for your shoulders,
my words for hello.

Your heartbeat rises through
the good earth to nod my flowers.
I breathed my name, for the wind
to tell you. Our messenger's laugh
love was no longer secret, except to us.

Our breath stolen, we had to breathe
each other. You would breathe my name
against your fingers — Blood oxygenated.
Our flesh in rebellion
allied with
natural forces to create our union.

No longer can love reach in private
jubilation. Gravity pulls us towards
the center, the wind rules our breath,
moved by tides we rise to beachheads,
driven through moist sands, blossomed
as petals, creation becomes a herald.

After this riot, on a quiet night,
stars — lightning bugs,
we acknowledge our reticence, taste the salt
tears, trails and good earth.
know all
is given by the gods. We
the fools who earn the prize.

0902
06-04-07
Newington, VA

Nation Builders

From the nest, they fell. So many raindrops,
they could not tell one from the other. Everyone
thought they were everyone else. Even when
they tried doing different things they were the same.
In the morning light, they were children of the dawn.

One took chalk and made marks on his cheeks. Another
took mud and smeared it across his forehead. The
birds took flight from the marsh;
the deer dashed over the ridge.

To let them know who they are, they were
allowed to wear their lives on their face. Some claimed
they were children of the night and were invisible
during the daytime. This allowed them to hunt better.

Others claimed the clay and shaped bowls,
walked farther from the streams because they had water.
Some hid under the leaves and stayed pale.
Everyone forgot about the day they rained to earth.

They discovered names. They used them to describe,
to define, to be different. They used them over and over,
most of them forgot what they meant until
only the poets and singers knew their power.

The Great One watched them and was amused.
At the same time, he shed a tear and valleys were flooded.
"They will take a long time to learn who they are.
Even longer to learn how to be one, just like the rain."
The Great One knew to love is to set free.

1707
12-26-17
Stafford, VA

SOME DAYS YOU KNOW YOU ARE DIFFERENT

She watched the flies on the other side
crawling on the screen door. Spotted
a deer come to a halt on the edge
where the wood teetered to a halt against the yard.
Somewhere inside she sought for a breath,
choked on a tear left from a summer just before
she became the woman she is learning to be.

There is no fine line where life says here you are
and there you were, or you wake up and know
"now I am." It creeps up on you and your parents are
the last ones to recognize it. It's a fight
sometimes.

The deer don't come by often enough
and the flies never leave.

It was a day where she had turned off everything else
after the coffee was made. Let memories drift across
the screen of her mind, see which ones caused a heartbeat.
Last summer had been about boys when
she had wanted a man. She couldn't tell you what one was.
But, she'd know. Like the heat of a summer day,
it encompassed all of you.

Last summer, she had unfolded her long legs,
let her wings fold in the fashion of hope,
found there were more eyes in a day than she remembered.
Spent more time in the sun
on a blanket
with sunglasses
protecting herself from the glare
of others looking too closely for comfort.

Sometimes she envied the deer.
Every summer she wanted to kill all the flies.

There was nothing good to be said about a mosquito.

1818
07-14-18
Stafford, VA

SORCERY IN TRAINING

We scrambled along the branches
sailing into adventures, searching horizons
held in the graceful pastoral streets of ticky-tac houses
packed divinely against the hills. Challenged
to climb as high as we could we swayed in the wind
knew that stars shimmered in our hair
as we dared the thunder to echo in our hearts.
As the last skinned knees faded with a forgotten summer —
we leaned against the gnarled knots, broken dreams,
tight-fisted hopes and boasted how we would conquer
the sports field, scientific wonders, and perhaps
find a better way to impress people than being
king and queen of the prom. After promising never to tell,
in a sudden spell of brazen innocence, we kissed.
I never told how broken I felt when your first date
wasn't with me or the rocks I kicked when you were pinned.

Magic follows its own time and once cast and forgotten
can be confused with miracles. College, life, and the movement
of planets take us into orbits where trees, skinned knees,
pirates, and dragons are left scattered on bedroom floors
behind closed doors and parent's best wishes. She slipped
into the shadows of my yesterdays and I was a laugh
she heard now and then when a distant view whispered.

Weather reports, promises, and umbrellas for
Just in case, the shelter of a bus stop stand,
rain -- a curtain -- suddenly you are alone.
The sudden burst through the flood, drenched,
a sudden pause, the look, the smile,

"It's you."

We unfolded into each other lives, found time to take time
and swing by a certain tree that still swayed in the wind
held breezes that whispered and raced through its leaves.
Let me and her leave with you to know that we lived
in the mad chaos of each moment with the heat of our love
the laughter of family and understanding that magic
is a constant creation in which we believe.

2143
06-03-16
Stafford, VA

SHE IS . . .

the drink waiting

cold cool fresh
a sudden shock

the bright morning full
beckoning awakened
to the heart

the tease of branches turning green
the wave wrapped around ankles
disappearing — the patient sand
a constant question, metaphorical

05-21-07
2239
Alexandria, VA

CATCHING UP

Crawled out of the covers, expected snow
got misty rain and fog lay in tatters across the lake.

The dog was ready.
Rain stopped on cue.

I feel the gravel push against the soles of my shoes. Ashen reeds,
pale ghosts against the brown leaves glistening with rain.

She stopped
at the top of the slope, a silhouette against the clouds.

We were ghosts in the valley. Walked through
banks of fog that drifted across the dam. I hoped she waited.

She laughed with recognition as we materialized out of the fog.
Hear her voice. A trilling harp weaves around the waking geese and ducks,
who wait for the sun to burn away the fog -- take flight.

When we joined her, she pointed down to the lake. The geese
gathered, a cacophony of honking; began to race and lift off,
broke through curtains of fog as they formed a vee. White light,
the morning sun climbed above the hill, shrouded in clouds.

Her arm twined with mine and the hatted head pressed against me.

The dog pulled on the leash. My love rose to tiptoes and kissed me on the chin.
I began to disappear into a sunny fog. Let my arms encircle her.
The dog raced about us, tied us tightly against one another, stumbling,
trying to stand still -- we found
silence in a kiss and a heartbeat.

Later, as the last shreds of morning lingered by the front door,
she let me know it was good I had caught up with her.
It was better together than to walk alone. I held on,
aware, lingering scents of cinnamon, nutmeg, and fall.

1:29 PM
11-27-12
Stafford, VA

POSTMORTEM OF A SUICIDE

No one will know when I die,
they will have stopped listening long ago.

In the end, history and regrets,
clarity that the light was a mirage,
potential will never pay the bills
and no matter how much they love you
you only hear about the last party.

Never be surprised by how self-serving
human beings are. Encapsulated —
at one point or another we are all
aggressive drivers, "Get out of my way, you..."

There will be no suicide note.
God is not controlling my last misadventure.
Karma is a future investment
and I am sure I don't have one.

If you are obvious, people want sublime; If you
are subtle, they demand clarity; Just cause you
choose to walk your path, doesn't guarantee
anyone will follow it
or even notice you're missing, unless you
owe them something.

Depression is not the killer, recovery is.

0013
06/08/09
Alexandria, VA

CHOCOLATE AND TANGERINE

Sand screams, footprints crushing crystals of rime into runes
cuneiform memories of sailors and mermaids, tales of silk trade.

Wind whips the sand till it starts to rub the face raw with ice
edged knives, coats pulled tight, heads turtle down into collars.

Doors burst open and humans clatter, chatter and tumble: a chaos
of greetings. The fire's sparks, crackles flames in a promise of heat.

Mugs steaming with hot chocolate and a bowl of tangerines
blossom on the dining room table as the outdoors is shed upon chairs.

Marshmallows melting and she looks over the rim, tongue darting to taste.
Remember when summer tumbled across the shore and she was tangerine.

Bikini promises wrapped around a chocolate tan, her hands against
the cheeks of your face and sliding around to pull close into tangerine rose.

The odors of innocent kisses, skin under fingers, sounds crashing on beaches
a moment tattooed and scalding the heart. Chocolate passion melts.

The skin of the tangerine is torn, pushed quickly aside and left on the table.
Each segment is relished allowed to explode upon the tongue. Memories

return without being called. The flush and rush of flavors, the odors recall:
she was tangerine and came just before the fall stole the heat of summer.

12:18 AM
02-17-15
Stafford, VA
during a snow storm

BEFORE WE SPOKE OF LOVE

Started with a conversation.
Your understanding insightful comments
brought me out of the shadows, tall thoughtful,
kept me at your feet. I studied your toes.
How easy it would be to create a story where
your toes were heroic, risked crossing abysses
carried calf and thigh, your wonderful
graceful sway of slender grasses.

I look up

your eyes hold me. I know I am seen
accepted and can no longer stand at the back
of the room, waiting to be forgotten.

All that is left is a song. Music can
hold all these worlds of you. The notes
allowed to rain -- a thousand fingers —
the magic of light holds your heart, so you
can know I will be, I am — the one who
hears all you would say. The one who
will learn all you can be.

09-28-13
01:54 PM
Celebrate, VA

CURSE MAINTENANCE

Too often —
in the shadows of our dreams,
stands the horror
we believe we are.
How is it
we believe we are broken?
* *
The child received
is so perfect
it is a miracle impossible to believe.
There they are
in your arms
part of you forever.
We curse and swear
out of fear
they may be too much like us
and suffer all the hell we have lived.
* *
I just wanted them to love me.
Not how I should be
would be
could be
just as I am.
I may be made of clay
but the hands that molded me were God's.

Can't my parents just celebrate
the gift I am?
If they can't,
I am only the curse.
I don't understand
how I was born broken
where no doctor can see.

1849
01-05-19
Stafford, VA

TWEENER

Spring can be such an awkward child.

She leaps into our arms and then
slips off our seat to stand at a distance
letting a chill settle on the air.
We pray for her return,
bitch about the shadows
cast by winter's memory.

Spring finally spreads her wings
lifts us into the arms of summer.
May all our children aspire to such feats.

1:12 PM
04-05-16
Stafford, VA

COUNSELING

The flip to the hair,
the cant of her hip
the stance. No chance
the thrash and crash
the chaos about her
would stop her attack.

Right up to the desk
asked for me by name.
Told me, she had heard,
I was the one. Or so
she proclaimed.

We work with families,
runaways, and the occasional walk-in.
I watched for tells before the tale.
She proclaims without a prompt,
"I am 12, look 16 and act 21."

"That's nice. What do you do for an encore?"
I responded, looking tired and a little bored.

"I'm headed for trouble. I promised
not to let it happen
heard you can help."

I sat up, said, "Let the intake begin.
If you got troubles
are willing to work,
then I got the program where you can win."

Masks, posturing, games, and mistrust.
Growing up is a pain
Expectations restraints
Love a complication when relationships turn
to dust. She was ready and geared to go
but just young enough not to know what roads
ran high and which ones ran low.
She wanted miracles and the grief to cease.

Her parents wanted help and couldn't believe
after three perfect daughters, what did this one
need. They were happy she'd come to me.

Counselors don't walk on water, nor turn it into wine.
Life's problems don't appear overnight.
Clean up takes scrubbing and discovery,
you got to find out what you want it to look like.

This tale had an ending after she argued and fumed,
did what needed to be done and still tried to prove
she could command the sun to rise and play the fool.
Growing up can be such a pain. There are no guarantees
and little you can believe if you want both eyes open
be able to set your course as you sail the seas.

Once she aged a little and learned direction and rules
were not put in place to keep her controlled. She saw what
she wanted to create out of her life. She saw she could
be in charge of what she made of herself and achieve
excellence which she declared when she made the grade.
We ended the sessions with her sure: she could act
intelligent and let others discover, cause she already knew,
just who she is.

12:49 PM
06-15-15
Stafford, VA

CONFESSIONS OF AN ANCIENT WITH SUICIDAL TENDENCIES

I get anxious.
It ain't the same as being afraid.
Afraid is something you can hold onto.
Aim at. Confront and defy.
Anxious just eats at you.

It wasn't until 1984 they would admit
men suffer from it.
It was so subtle only women could have it.
Men were rocks who couldn't admit to cracks.
They still don't call it anxiety. It's PTSD's.
It is simple, what no one wants to see,
it eats you alive.
You either find an addiction to hide in
or kill yourself by thirty, a few carry on.
Maybe, we are not the lucky ones.

I get anxious.
I make jokes. People say they are inappropriate.
They keep me alive. Let me love when
love seems like an impossible dream.
I want to scream.
I was taught not to make a scene.
Anxiety is an emotional itch.
Yeah, like poison ivy.
You can't really itch it.
If you do, you will scratch till you're raw.

Repressed, suppressed, depressed
what a fucking mess.
All I hear is get over it.
You get taught that you shouldn't need
and soon that becomes: You are not needed.
Death follows or you learn to say, "fuck 'em."

As a spirit, I am basically a very joyful person.
It is probably the reason I have survived to write this.
If you have read this far, you are either very caring
or you know what hell is because you live there.

Anxiety is not the disease, it is only a symptom.
It is a result of abuse disguised as correction.
It is being asked to endure when horrid things happen
that no one should experience;
then asked to remain silent cause no one wanted to hear.
Is caring so hard? Is it so hard we live withdrawn
watch our children, our families, our loves, and lovers
kill themselves over and over again.
I have heard fear called
False Expectation Appearing Real.
I am anxious.
I don't always know what the truth is.
It is killing me.
The hardest part of writing this is not to have it be
one continuous run-on sentence.
I am drowning and no one can see me running out of breath.

0952
08-27-18
Stafford, VA

Cause There Is Poetry

The wheat was reaped, silage folded back
into the heart of the soil. Harvest canned
wood split and the last turn taken to see
to the fence. Leaf loose and lark flown.
Where can you hear the music
but in a poem?

She was slender and a wonder at home.
He was stocky and broad, a worker at heart. She
watched him leave his house in the morn. Come
home grimy and tired as the sun went down.
He felt her eyes and loved her smile; wanted to share
his cares his home, but how could he tell her
except in a poem.

Feelings rise like waves come to shore. Days
pass and the night fills horizon's store. We grow,
lad and lass, till we create families of our own
or as time passes, we come to know how to be
alone. Art enters, a whisper to the soul.
No matter the form it takes, to speak of it
is a poem.

Poetry catches what lives in the heart
lets meaning catch the eye as it speaks to the soul;
gives us ways to share feelings, turn
to the unknown and dare to challenge it —
because we know we can speak of it
caught in the light and verse of a poem.

946
02-09-17
Stafford, VA

Not too Long, but Long Enough

i.

Dusk comes when darkness
is finally empty. You can
hear the breath of the shadows.
Dawn, for all attempts at subtlety,
is heard as soon as it enters —
an awakening of trumpets.

ii.

It is on the third day of hiking
the mind collapses. There is
nothing more to say.
A world, whose voice you had
forgotten, opens
within you.

iii.

After all the hugs, when
the heart was no longer
a flurry of wings seeking flight —
the fingers trace the lips
words held like one's breath
so the spell will not be broken.

iv.

The infinite curls up in a memory;
waits for the moment
when eternity cuddles up to us.
The blossoms along its path
lead us to where awe mingles with love
Faith becomes the steed
we ride.

1:08 PM
05/26/14
Stafford, VA

ADAM DISCOVERS EDEN, TOO

She knows when the wind
blows from my room; when
I visit the moon, stare
down upon her; let my ocean
sink quickly into her sands.

I measured the distance:
my heart to hers. It is a
step away. I trip ~
spilling onto her floors,
evaporate too quickly to memory.

We know, there is no reason.
Love grows despite the season.

We abandon the day

leave names scrawled on sidewalks.
Nobody is fooled. We are left
dealing with the impossible,
call to the other
say we are fools.

1815
09/02/07
Alexandria, VA

IT WAS ONLY YESTERDAY . . .

1.
I hear the wind chimes — still.
Breeze about to shift, even the birds
hold their peace, the warning of buoys, distant,
fold their clangor into the disappearing night.
She joins me on the verandah,
slipping out of the shadow of the house,
a whisper on my neck, two hands
on my shoulder keeping me from floating off
as the breeze begins again and silence is lost.

2.
She smiles, her fingers comb
the hair on my son's head, plays with a wave.
He tries to push her hand away.
Cries out as she grabs him and hugs him.
His protests make me laugh.
We only resist love when we are sure
it will never stop. I can
only smile remembering why I started
loving her.

3.
I am huge because she is tiny.

4.
The pink tip of her tongue caught
between her teeth. She stops and pushes
the glasses back up on her nose. Calls me
over to assist. Thanks me. Then leans against
me. I am never as strong as her regard makes me.
It is in the tiniest of moments, fireflies of love
where joy takes seed. Often, when I am by myself
trying to get something done, they blossom.
I have to pause and inhale the aroma before it is gone

1417
01-19-10
Alexandria, VA

FIRST LESSON

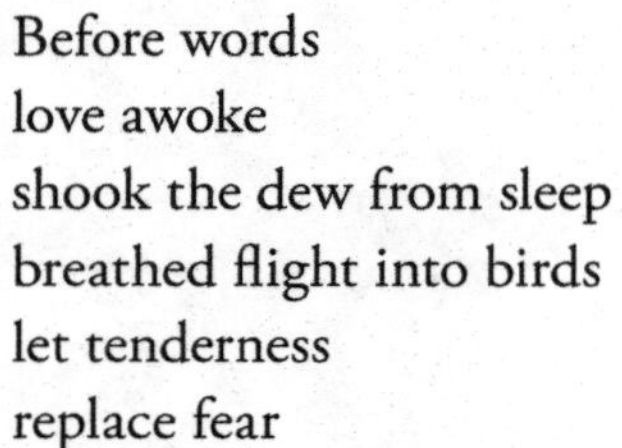

Before words
love awoke
shook the dew from sleep
breathed flight into birds
let tenderness
replace fear
created laughter
so we can
remain sane

1347
05-03-17
Stafford, VA

TAKE THE POT DOWN, PLEASE

"Be careful, when washing, the
teapot." She leaned over took
my hand holding the cloth, "You
have to be gentle.
It's too easy to wash away
all the history that sleeps inside."

My grandmother: gracious
mannerly — full of understanding
God's gifts, clear
there was a definite right and wrong
which she knew for every occasion.
But with me, she also shared
her sense of magic and ability
to see fairies when the right breeze
turned a leaf or a flurry of rain
let you hear them run across the roof.

She knew, in the calmness of evenings
when steam hung over the cup of tea,
how to stir the stray leaves left after
the tea ball was removed, whisper
secrets revealed
what many saw as coincidence.

"The world has an order," she told me.

As we enjoyed our tea, warmed
our fingers on hot cups,
listened to the house whisper its joy,
felt the folk draw nearer to see
the secrets in the leaves, "See that ripple!
A sprite just stole a taste from yours."

Because of her, I know
the magic of tea.

"Care to join me in a cup?"

1816
04-14-12
Stafford, VA

CREWEL POINTS

Pulling the lace shawl about her,
she points to the snow, "Winter
has come." Trees would not know
their nakedness, nor how to shiver
without her insights.

Firs bow, drop their basket of whites
when teased by the wind. Children
huddle at the stop
morning sheds grays.
School Bus fumes up to them.
Motorists stop, tap steering wheels
steam up the glass anticipating.

She watches
from her window. "We didn't use to
have to rush so. Children need more
time to play. The sledding hill stays empty
too often. I miss the laughter."

She never
has the TV on
when guests come.
It would be rude.
Tells me —
"People have lost the art of conversation."

Every visit, I see her blue eyes –
clear as a sharp winter day. Her skin
grows transparent. It's as if she will
become a ghost and haunt us with reminders.
She is more certain every day of what is right;
how we have forgotten the spirit of holidays.

She tells me old people should not have to suffer
from arthritis. There are times when
I think I must protect her. One stiff breeze —
suddenly, she would be gone.

I count each day as a gift.
She will not hear any of it.
Tells me, "Life is to be lived.
All of it."

I came over one morning.
The cat greeted me at the door.
The light was on in the living room.
She was tucked up in the armchair,
book on her lap. It looked like
she had just nodded off.

Even after the service
in the quiet of day's end
when all the birds have gone to branch,
I can feel her at my shoulder
reminding me, "Posture is everything.
"Stay present," she says, "Life is
too precious to miss. Any of it."

I can see solitary footprints,
fresh snow from last night.
Should be unsullied, but she dropped by.

5:48 PM
02-04-13
Porter Library, VA

WARRIOR CHIEFS

We, children of wind and rain, left
the sidewalks, the hard pavements of decision,
avoided front lawns and all the proper garden plots.

Lifting dew-drenched leaves to our lips
we let the silver moonlight captured
in these whispers of water make our inner
journeys rich beyond anyone's dreams.

Enjoying the elasticity of clay slip between
our toes and blossom in buttery red colors,
we let the banks of the rapid-running river
become our playground as we molded
the clay into monoliths, basilisks
turmoil and trouble to be flattened
by the heroic armies we led across the land.

Boys caught, brinks-men of pretense —
we turned the river into an ocean, filled
the air with the magnificence of dragons.
We were no longer arrows of might,
but metamorphosed into wizards, whose magic
made the earth tremble and the air shimmer
with doorways, we would use to transport
us away into the dens of thieves, where
riches lay waiting for the plucking.

In the distance, like the drone of warplanes,
we heard the beginning of highway's nightmare.
Nodding sagely, laughing occasionally —
simply to expose our bravery.

Blood brothers, tribal warriors, we allowed the night to be
pulled back from the crying sun. We heard
our mothers' call shimmer through
the fierce climate of our desires.

The echoes shattered.
We shrunk
watched blood heroically earned
become caked streaked slashes of mud.
Dinner called.

All we held to be true crumbled back behind our tired eyes.
A breeze lifted and raced along the path we watched
cut through the trees back to the sky. We return.
down sidewalks through doorways. Washed
in tubs and sinks, the last stink
dragons down drains and
into the quiet caves
we would rest
in the glory
of our
dre
am
s.

6:56 PM
01-08-12
IAD

SELF-TAUGHT

We learned to play and weave a game of shadows,
tank tops, tie-dyed rainbows and fence post birches
marching along the river bank. Secret lockets lost
in the untraceable spaces 'tween rocks and river;
woven with tales of Indians, haunted canoes
and flights of geese suddenly becoming maidens feathering oars.

This dance of magic footprints before we knew each other.

Pinecone blossoms, wisps of smoke 'bout black seed,
a frozen wafer of intangible lightness, we spilled
out of summer brown and otter races,
grew through the flickering fire lights, cricket cries
and lightning bug lanterns beneath the starry black candelabras.
We skied and snow-shoed back trails along wood and blackberry tangles;
shadows and memories holding our laughter as we puffed smoke signals
into the crisp cold. Best friends, partners, we explored our landscapes
promised heroic outcomes and knew each other's dreams.

Perhaps, it is the fault of the willows,
the privacy of falling hair and roots like arms
the tangle of our shared memories and fruits ripening
before we had outgrown our long-legged coltish romps,
kite races, and the sweat of hot summer days driving us
to dive, naked, into the black pond waters reflecting a white summer sun.

If she hadn't tickled my cheek with pussy willow;
if I hadn't learned the taste of honeysuckle on her lips,
the way they glistened when moist with laughter.

Innocence is best
savored as a memory.

6:38 PM
12-29-11
IAD

Atlas Tries to Understand Metaphysics

Let me find where summertime is
against the ache of my belly,
the drums of springtime pulsing in my groin,
the cycle of seasons ripening in my hair —
aromas: sage, lavender, rosemary, cut grass,
sounds: owls, arguing blue jays, the snap, and scratch
branches against the house and I will know

what pulls my strings, sings the tunes I dance to.

These hands of my environment till me, roll
over my skin, fill me with seed; women stand
naked in my rivers, sit against rocks, pound the laundry,
laugh, spit, scratch — be women with women
children run through the jungle
the women's legs and snatching hands.

Rain and war, guns and thunder, bullets and blood, bombs and floods
the soaking ground absorbs all it is given.
Man's hate sows me with salt,
leaves me barren,
pounds me with desolation so no family can blossom;
leaves me stark desert looking for kisses.

A breeze slips around a corner and I hear old
men rocking on porches, telling lies to young
men, who try to see tomorrow before
yesterday is forgotten and no one remembers what has been done.

I feel her clutch me, kiss my neck, curl against my spine.
In the morning, she laughs
washes my back and I feel
the strength that holds babies, scrubs floors.
She looks me straight in the eye.

Tells me I can never quit.

Feels me quiver with the sharp edge of winter
wraps me in a blanket
wraps me with herself
takes my shivers into her
stirs them into her magma.

If summer is a season pressed against me,
then I would be foolish to go courting in the chill
winter, where snows smear outlines and leave me empty.

A universe unfolds
every time I begin
scratching the itch of creation.

6:21 PM
01-10-12
IAD

SNOW

White silk has its own textured voice
as sheets whisper with cross threads
gliding against each other.
Tease the skin with memories and warm hopes.
Sunlight's dance upon the billowing froth --
coverlets, linens, pillows that rise and fall
across the bed; she casts an eye from pallet
white to window's empty vision.
Remembers the softness of darkness,
the passion still scenting the room,
her feeling of fullness.
Not ready to leave the recently born memories,
unwilling to cast aside the last sensual flavors
from the night before, not quite ready to let water
slip across her skin like his fingers —
she lets the silence fill her, craft the ache.
Her longing becomes a song.

She is filled with the whispers of snow upon the sill,
his last words and a kiss that still melts inside her.

4:15 PM
03-22-11
Alexandria, VA

HYLAS

When Hercules left,
and I wove my echoes around the Nymphai
kisses and laughter. I hid my tears in splashes
wiped my lashes against lily pads and stirred a breeze.

You called.
I answered.
You only heard yourself.

How often has love been the wave
you charged through,
drove your ship up the face and brow pierced?

You wonder at the storms.

You stand alone
never hear me. I call and call
you smile
tell those at the mast of the echoes.

Many thought I was a thief of dreams
wrapped in the flesh of nyads and Nymphai.
If only they had known,
if I could do more than echo
the wind and the memory of kisses.

These centuries, when the spring pond memory,
now only the wind and I howl along.
We stood on the face of waves
echoed the cries of sailors.
They never knew, couldn't hear
how much I
longed to rescue them from their struggles;
become the hands upon their arms
footsteps on the planked fore deck.
Oh to race up the main mast and look out at the far and wide.
I open my chest to the Sword
the gods only laugh and I must
echo.

2:43 PM
09-28-14
Stafford, VA

A RAKE

Leaves fall through the morning
mist, sails teasing traces of dawn.
Light tastes fawn, magenta, carmine, lemon.
They puddle upon the matte green,
leaves woven into earthy rainbows.
Wisps of mist shredded slip into quivers of shadow.
Kisses, cool from the autumnal night,
surrender to the passion of a last summer surge.
Sol dances across a clear ache of blue
teased by cotton candy stretches of clouds.

People declare, shading their eyes,
"What a beautiful day," unbutton
the top two, wave hands like casting a spell
before their neck and declare they love this time of year.

When the last lantern finds its resting place
upon the end of the highway, mountain — a pedestal
a sigh escapes as the headlights are switched on porch
lights beam across black grass.

The moon tickles its way across a neck,
creates a chiaroscuro landscape
hides an ocean of stars and stirs dreams.

First freeze is in the air —
even as the earth starts to keep its distance
the Light never rejects its love

7:38 PM
10-25-12
Stafford, VA

THE HUNT

The thunder of summer shimmers
the heat and promises of relief
even as we sip ice teas
tease the heat with glances.

Sunbonnets, the snort of horses,
Middleburg ready to enjoy the leaps.
Creak of saddles, shadows of jodhpurs
hard riding hats gathered
a rack of billiards on matte green.

Southern accents this far north
pretense and money.
Hospitality is hard to come by
without knowing the right stores,
which finger to curl and what rein to grip.

A ray of sunshine pierces the tent of magnolias.
Pastel colors in silk and chiffon
flutter like butterflies and impish children
race off with sweets as the crowd sighs
applauds the feats of horsemanship.

Her white gloved hand shows me
the flesh exposed as she turns her palm
down upon her knee. She takes off
her summer hat, fans herself with a program,
lets the sunlight race across her cleavage.
Looks me straight in the eye,
"I don't know. Sipping this sweet iced
tea, just makes me hotter."

Her laughter dances across a field
where horses race and leap, vying for a lead.

06:56 PM
01-09-16
Stafford, VA

PROMISE

Whispered
"Hush, I will know how you really feel
when the morning wakes in your eyes."
Drowsy, we had drunk
so deeply of each other,
we climbed into the cave of each other's
heartbeats and let the night
crumble against us, as we held on
to that last moment when we were one.

1341
06-07-17
Stafford, VA

THE WORLD WAS CAST ADRIFT

I woke up with the taste
her words on my fingertips:
Crisp tang of apples threaded
with the bite of brandy,
a last cigarette, trailing
smoke, a path into the night sky.
Her hands, open
beckon me to let silence
still my tongue,
follow the flight of sparrows,
become tangled like a kite's tail
in the open capillaries of trees.
I rise from my bed,
leave dreams struggling
gasping for air.
I stand in the window light
watching my skin
go from pink to white.
Wonder what kisses I will find
in the caress of the breeze.
There is magic abroad.
I can feel her weight pressing
like a memory trying to be remembered.
As if a bubble of history escaped death
burst into my present and set off alarms.
We are remnants of forever.

Unpuzzling our connection
as the gears of the "Great Machine"
keep manufacturing a more mundane
rational explanation for why
I can taste her meaning
when she whispers a breeze past my ears.

9:27 PM
11/29/08
Alexandria, VA

PENNY WISE, DOLLAR SHORT

I woke up to you
a day late, after
all the "I love you's"
were faded, drooping
ready to be tossed
water poured down the drain.

Sometimes,
real love is planted
so deep; it doesn't sprout
until after the romance
is tattered by the rain.

I know you're packed,

all the tears sealed behind
goodbyes. "I got no right,"
I can hear it
even as I ask you to remain.

10:45 PM
4/20/10
Alexandria, VA

HOW TO SPEAK MANY LANGUAGES

what's more beautiful than a woman wearing poetry?

-- shadowhand

I found you imprinted with your festival of words.
They would fall syllables at a time across my lips
tease my tongue, find me tasting a verb you had cherished.
I know we have filled evenings recreating
subtle and ancient dialects, mixed phrases from many cultures
found methods of making distinctions that opened our souls
wholly new ways of being in each other's presence.

Steal our tongues, our fingers become loquacious
subtly competent in verbiage that hides in sinew.
Deprive us of touch and we will create dances
our eyes will find hypnotic and a lexicon will grow anew.
Music lives in the beat of our blood, every beat
layered with innuendo. The poetry that flows out of life
lives as long as humans desire to be alive, love
be gods of their own creation, and celebrate its sharing.

5:38 PM
5/30/13
Stafford, VA

TREES ARE THUNDER IN THE FOG

When we are liquid, dropping kisses to create ripples,
shores catch us, take the diamonds that dance in
the froth to hang on the leaves of roses.
Tomorrow is born out of an echo found in this moment.

Intimacy greets surrender lingers on fingers
pressed against lips as walls tumble:
legs unfold from shadows, neck to crane
the charms of your origami turn Luna into a lantern.
The hands of lovers often are birds in flight.
Evaporated into the sky, rained back upon ourselves:
we, for all our freedom, are caught in the cycles:
this world reflected as it echoes itself; we are
current and stream, dream sang true.

Caught in the stillness of an echo,
the fog betrays itself, smearing
its own reflection. Kisses surrendered:
rain feeds the roots of a blossom.

High tide, the moon's maiden swirls her skirts.

10:46 PM
11/01/07
Alexandria, VA

LEARNING TO CHOOSE

Her memories slipped out of keyholes
slid down banisters, danced
with their eyes closed and finally got tangled
where dreams became the backbone of seduction.

Living was never complicated, its creation
a blessing that unfolded into blossoms over years.
The enticement, the touching as one awakened
to every fiber's unique speech — this, alone,
was worth every second of study. Memories
often, create the spark to reawaken a fire.

It was worth the time, she thought as she brushed
out the night's eddies, uncurled the combers,
remembered the man. He never toyed, never
acted as if he knew her before she spoke. He
enjoyed, tasted and played with her, so they
discovered each other in the process of learning
how they could be when together, partners.

She enjoyed the weight of her braid, the thought
he could create a new world as he undid it, joined
her in its magic and wrote new words
for the worlds they created in dusky reds,
alabaster, ivory and ebony nights to the fresh
spill of clear light on a reborn day.

12:06 PM
3/29/13
Stafford, VA

TO EMILY: AS ONLY I KNEW HER

I broke bread in the first light;
scraped the smeared yolk from the plate.
Your shadow stretched across the sill;
the shifting origami of darkness told of your approach.

We created these rough diamonds
untooled, unset, unopened in our hearts.

Later, the hands of history
and memory's instruments would facet them
allowing their precious beauty to spill their light
across the paths, we wandered
to understand what maybes were left.

The snow caked on your feet.
First, pans of cold water;
then, my hands hold them
whispering massage, but afraid
they will shatter in my grasp.

I feel you cover the sun
burn the edge of my ear with a kiss.

The laughter diminishes with distance.
I wash away the stains on the cement,
clean the dirt out of the carpet,
but feel your kisses
framed on every wall, after
I walk through any doorway.

I know the years the tides
the darkness gathers.

12:05 AM
05-25-12
Stafford, VA

CRANES & KITES

Imagine this cloth -- space.
Hands of an origami master
make creases and folds,
bring the far near. Time,
a whim, only measures age
becomes but a feather on a crane.

I would measure kisses
by tablespoons of wind.

I become quiet, you fall
into me. I am a tree, entangling
your kite, after it has
soared with the birds.
Our hands meet and become oceans.
Currents surge forth,
new blood. We are twin
stars with the gravity of light.

Storms: lightning in touch
thunder in pulse.

12:55 PM
6/28/08
Alexandria, VA

GRAMMAR

I am an unfolding sentence
parsed against a page that is inebriated with ink.

Words gather in the web of my fingers,
the chatter of a thousand thoughts
seeking replies by any means possible,
every alphabet languaging itself in my blood.

I find a spiral; let it form inside me
and I turn and turn and turn
feel the vortex gather speed as
the center remains calm
producing meaning when chaos
consumes all structure.

The gods had no choice,
jealousy and envy were destroying them.
Heaven was too much of a good thing
and its music was frothed with poetry.
Love stepped out of a wavefront.
Meaning became a story
about having and not having.
How silly we are in creating scarcity
when love is
infinite.

I found myself picking up the clutter of my history.

Disappearing in the resolution of answers
like rain falling on a page of watercolors.

(Problems are washed away.)

She presented herself.
In a moment of speechlessness, the poetic justice of silence
opened the night
and forgot to unlock the sun
as we became all that two are
in the formula of One.

0107
11-03-15
Stafford, VA

RAISING SAND DOLLARS

Hands behind my head, sun in my eyes
a shadow crosses and in the darkness
your eyes flash green and greedy.

We are together and separated by a body
ready to be touched, stirred like mystic waters.
I hear your knees crunch in the sand
as the sun once again heats me to blindness.
You shake the sand from my feet, laughing
as I fight the light to see what you find funny.

I am beached and you approach an ocean
wave after wave, hands and body swarm across
this tender island, remnant of a volcano, a love.
Smooth as a seal, skin kisses skin, little wavelets
shudder quickly between us, bringing laughter
small kisses, eyes shining, shadows letting moisture
shimmer on all too wonderful lips arcing down,
an echo of surf: echo of wonder and joy.

Your heartbeat tattoos against my chest.
Consistency of what we share: Celebration
togetherness brings to life. Here in the heat
we melt slowly, puddles of ecstasy,. Troubles
woes stripped of consequence and meaning.
Left to flap nonsense into the breeze. We are
free to allow the day to enter us with light.

Once we stood in separate towers.
We cried out desperation; we struggled with need.
Now in the wash of waves, we have fallen
naked into each other's heart. Now
for once, we become welcome to each
heart in a feast of serenity, bliss and love.

6:16 PM
March 29, 2015
Stafford, VA

GROWING PINIONS

There is a poem fluttering against
my heart, taking on the pulse, dancing
with blood cells, whispering
scabrous thoughts, until
I am forced
to respond.

My long-legged retort is full of spine.
The ram-rod lightning of broad recognition.
I share visions. I employ analogy.
The magic that words possess
becomes the seed of tangled forests
tied up in moonlight and ragged dreams.

Footsore and possessed,
the miles hitchhiked, allowed to resonate
with the hum of tires and folklore born
in glove boxes, maps and all the paraphernalia
used before technology shattered the treasures
tied up in the bandanas of haphazard accomplishment.

I fill my emptiness with liquor and mead,
allow gods to gather at the hearths beside black holes.
Legends are forged in the flames,
heroes formed in the recounting of battles
in the loneliness around the heart, romance is born.

I am written and the poetry of me
is never to be found tattooed in plain sight.
When I die, the song that stirred the words
will not disappear in the ashes of my temple.

Flight, exploration, the opening of new horizons
is where my words lie -- unfettered, unbowed
ready to join with those who dream and make it real.

Midnight
11-05-15
Stafford, VA

CARPENTER

Seasons are cyclical.
My house is structural. Built
to withstand the rotation of time.

The swirl of her pleated skirt
left trails in my sawdust. The smile
refracted the sunlight. I missed
hitting the head squarely and the nail
bent. Craftmanship's constructions
meet the destruction caused by
courtship. She never slipped
stubbed a toe or let frustrations show
while the dust flew and the wonder of my house
grew. The kitchen divine, the living space
sublime and she declared it all so fine once
she had the time to decorate accordingly.
Then I realized I belonged to her
not me. Matrimony is not recorded
at the courthouse as a form of freedom.

Spring came and we planted well. Summer arrived
as the kids grew high and the house became
a home, full of magic spells, special smells
and the twist of desires, fires and mother's
sure hands on the reins. As fall approached, the kids
stayed in touch and came home for special occasions.
Now a grandma, she grew larger with love
now that she had so many to share it with. I made wooden
puzzles and games, rearranged the shop so I could
never stop making rocking cradles and horses for each
child that arrived. Where once we were family with friends.
Now we had grown to be many homes filled with love.

The winter came and she took to bed. The dust grew
in corners and the stove cold from lack of use. The children
came in whispers instead of on wings of laughter. The grands
as mice at the foot of the bed. She smiled and coughed,
said prayers and asked for blessings to warm her heart
make it possible to leave the bed. Possible fled
leaving impossible in its stead. The morning crept
past curtains and fell upon the spread that no longer
moved with her breath. Instead, the quiet like a shadow
filled in what had once been full of laughter. Death
is understood long before the tears, the sermon, the burial
left the bed, the room, the house empty as we wept.

Life has its cycles, no matter how well we build,
they move about us, whether we choose to acknowledge or notice
each as it comes and goes. I stir the dust on my workbench,
I remember the laughter that came with each nail I bent.
I built the house and we filled it.
I built the house and she gave birth to every reason for calling it home.
I built this house and time's rotation has left it empty
me alone. The children come calling but have lives of their own.
My hands can't hold hammers, the house gathers dust,
the season's never stop turning and I am left with memories.
Us

0027
04-17-16
Stafford, VA

ANOTHER DAY AT 5825

I can hear you. Your footsteps sinking
into the carpet then padding on the kitchen floor.
The water running as you rummage
through the cabinets for a glass. Ice
the cracking sound it makes as water hits it.
The path of your return till the stairs creak.
I enjoy the sound of you coming closer.

You stop and watch me from the door.
Your smile lights your eyes. Everything
so ordinary, every day. Some of the best times
are letting my senses fill with how you move
through the moment, create the texture. I can
enjoy listening for the shifts in breathing as you
read a book, the light on your fingers turning
the page and pushing your glasses
back up on your nose. Stick your tongue
out at me for watching so closely.

The laughter in kisses, the lingering thought
fingers dragging across a shoulder as you
leave the room during a commercial.
You shush my protests, as you sit on my lap.
The shadows fill the room pressuring us
with reminders of how we need to turn on
the lamp, giggle and return to our discussions
leading nowhere.

1656
May 30, 2009
Alexandria, VA

MY TEACHER

He grabbed my little finger
pulled himself to a standing position
before he knew he wasn't supposed to.
The nurse told me he was too young.
He was six hours old and already
collecting criticism for being ahead of his time.

Never heard a word I said, but I watched
him copy the way I stood and my expressions
flitted across his face before he discovered
his own. I never saw a mirror that taught
me as much as he could about who I am.

"They are our greatest teachers,
if we are willing to learn the lessons
they place before us." I heard the therapist
summarize my thoughts before I heard
what I had been trying to tell myself.

How can I, someone caught in his own dilemmas,
make such a profound difference in a life.
I listen to how much I am talking to myself
when I am trying to steer him right. More and more
I find a stillness where I love him without words.

We rethreaded the front axle on his bike
so we could fit the nut back on and he could
ride free. I let him do all the work and earned
the biggest smile for being there while he did it.
I knew then, I had no more excuses for not succeeding.

11:33
06-24-09
Alexandria, VA

NEIGHBORWOOD

The slow spiral about a thermal,
wings spread, unmoving, except
when tips curve, flex caress, a shift in the flow

A feather falls —
a dream set free —
shiftless upon the rivered winds.
Its gyrations, a graceless counterpoint
to the beauty of flight. Still, my child
races through the grasses disturbs crickets,
dragonflies, and frogs to capture what has fallen.

Summer hums with insects, reptiles
animals that seek to adapt to suburbia,
the clatter of trash cans, sudden acts of wildness
along creeks hiding out at the back end of the yard.
Running water is a siren, wet rocks and mud
enticing (play sets all too formal). The wild,
a comma in the sentence of ramblers,
a better home for dreams growing children.

My son stands atop the rise
feather clutched, high above his head.
Breeze reaches out tousles his hair.
I can hear his laughter
the colors seem to shimmer.
He runs towards me,
my private wild man
glorying in his success.

I lift him up into my arms.
He tickles my face with the feather.
It is time to go.
Dinner is waiting.
He looks up at me
waves his plume,
sure he can do anything
when the next adventure calls.

12:59 PM
05-18-12
IAD

MIGRATION OF THE HEART

Out of the gray mornings,
where clouds lie against the water,
low bellies of infinite plainness —
the dark line of horizon is erased —
leaving only forever to hold
the clouds of our breath,
the mittened palm swallowed
by my black gloves, trembled
against the cold quiet.

Child of mine, deep in the wings —
these feathers of coruscating color
describing tern, mallard, snow geese
resting on the glass lake —
rushing suddenly, tiny gales of energy,
becoming part of the sky,
turns to me, in a moment of wonder,
"How do they know where they are going,
if they have never been there before?"

I wrap my arms across his chest.

He leans back against the envelope of flesh

holding me to the earth. "The same way
you know which colors are hot and which
ones are cool. The same way your laughter
makes the color of my love a rainbow."

1040
12/07/09
Dulles International Airport (IAD)

Berries for Breakfast

Barefoot and fancy-free with a touch of mud
upon the cheek, you wandered
back across the creek. The bucket of berries
half eaten on the way home. The birds, still
cheering the laughter that danced
out of your heart. Tales of gypsy queens
magicians lurking behind each tree, you told
me all the trials and travails you
suffered for a few fresh berries dressed in dew.
"Only half a pail," you cried, "I got
least a half of pail because I drove
a hard bargain with the elves who rescued me."
I could only laugh and wipe the tears from my eyes.
Gave you a hug and emptied
the berries into the batter. Waffles, Belgian-style
berries, and love covered in maple syrup to smooth
the path to the tum. Your face lit by the sun
as it created halos through the window pane.
Spring is dancing through the last of winter.
The creek along the meadow laughs
across rocks and branches as it fills with melted
snow. The sun has found its heat again, I am
captured you surround me with a dance of smiles
My daughter is full of magic --
I am warm with how she shares her gifts.

12:07 PM
01/18/07
Alexandria, VA For Ashley

NOR'EASTER: THE STORM'S A-COMMIN'

Winter has its own words. Rake
of a northeastern wind strips the
skin so we pull up scarf
don gloves and insulate ourselves from the world.

I brace myself at the door, long
to return, find myself nested against her,
burning away the coils of starlight tossed
across her bed so she will not take
me and feast upon my heart. I must
stoke the fire till our skin is tender from heat,
let her magic swirl about me until she
cries out, runs ragged claws down my back
arcs hard enough to throw planets off course.

then, simmers
watchful

as sleep steals into the room and banks
us against each other so the room shimmers
against every cold kiss the night might seek to bring.
Winter's sun pierces our shadows, breaks
open my eyes. She pulls against me, moans.

As I close the front door the black leaves
swirl against the stoop, I pull on my gloves,
pull down my hat and curse all —
this winter day and its iridescent icicles.

1628
11-04-12
Stafford, VA

A STRANGER

Black Rose blossoms upon the horizon.
Out of the origami shadows from the hills
he comes, a pace with walking stick
there to carry weight, befriend the journey.

Here, where silence chases away
the creaks of my rocker
lays abed with my history and shadows.
I rise in all the ache of my sunsets
let the door swing wide and light stutters
across the porch. A wind stirs
chases leaves across the lawn.
Has he seen me?
Invitations in the darkness
hope nested in a fortress.
Soon even in the shallow pools of moonlight,
there is nothing to tell.

He has passed.

1301
05-02-17
Stafford, VA

A WORD TO THE WISE

My neighbor came by the other day,
told me he had married the winds;
he was out for a walk until she blew herself out.
Her cyclones, hurricanes led to calling names
and water spouts, when doing the dishes, were not
a time for talking, but one for getting out.

He winked at me, started chewing on a piece of grass,
mused, "Oh, but when the tropical breezes come in
off the shore . . ." The gleam in his eye spoke volumes.

Told me once about being a sailor. Said all the tales
never told enough and were calmed so landlubbers
could believe them. He never tried keeping a lawn,
the yard was pond and rocks and sand so wind tossed
it was impossible to dream it had ever been walked upon.

Neighbors talked, and don't they always, about the music
that came from the rocks about the pond that sang you to sleep
making you dream about appointments you had to keep.
Wives always complained the following day about all the calls
their husbands made to their mothers and old girlfriends,
like some madness had overtaken them and they had to
heed the call.

I always could tell when the clouds grew dark
he was out walking nearby. I guess, as he said, she needed
time to herself so she could calm the furies goading her head.
Sometimes its "yes dear" to keep them near
other times it is giving them space to tat the lace,
decide on the length of thread. This is a crazy neighborhood,
full of Norns, Furies and other ladies of deed and dread,
but I call it home and where I love to lay my head.

1809
05-14-17
Stafford, VA

SYMBIOTIC

When the night is draped, the dust from the wings of stars
settles, Morpheus spirals the helix of his cloak 'round
his slender needle of a body. He comes knocking,
pierces the certitude of sleep. Follows the steps

down, the steady pace of breath, the cellar
where memories are folded dusty, left scattered on workbenches,
between sharp edges — planes, chisels, knives, saws —
all the teeth used to gouge and shape the timber of experience.

Morpheus reaches into the closets, behind the Sunday best,
drags out the old yarn twined with silk thread,
weaves the tale of chimney sweeps and princesses
through golden flakes of sunlight that melts
a frazzled morning of running late for work …

catch the bus, the running deer, the Great Dane
van, still panting in a desert gray with exhaust
steady, at work climbing the stairs and fire escapes
spirals and helix, around and around, never fast enough
out of breath as I come to a landing panting and shaking,
hands-on knees, Then, I see her, out of the corner of my eye,
a dream – the One. Hear the trumpets!
the angels sing. Morpheus hums along, feeling strong.
wake my partner with my efforts to sing along.
A ship is leaving the harbor and the fog, sounding its horn.
The alarm is going off and I have already worked my shift.
Morpheus smiles, glows from this fine meal of hopes. Bed
is empty. A light glows around the shade. I hear a song again,
where have I heard it? The bedroom door swings open …

"Coffee," she says, " you must get up or you will be late."
Smell the coffee, love the feel of her kiss. I don't hear
the hiss because the birds are so loud, Morpheus
pulls away turning gray in the, oh so bright, sun.

1337
4-21-12
IAD

CAN YOU HEAR THE ICE CRY AGAINST SPRING'S ARRIVAL?

I watched the willows dance against a breeze
Remembered the moments when she spun
a tendril of willow tears about her stared
down at me, growled, became a stripper prancing.
Slipping in and out of shadows, leaving
the branch behind like a discarded boa.

Love was laughter, touching and
dreams so big we would fly with them.

She rocks in the living room, hums
suddenly gets up and dances to a song
thirty years old and I try to catch ... before she falls.
She called the police twice to catch the prowler
called my name while she hit me. The tears
I cried not from being hit by her butterfly blows.

I remember her catching our child,
singing lullabies angels would gather to hear,
cooking things up in the kitchen, her experiments
we loved to test, so quick with a compliment,
so fast to change anyone's frown to a smile

I have heard everything the doctors have to say.
I have read all the stories and know all the signs.
My heart will never understand as she grows more frail,
becomes a memory in her own flesh. I look at
the garden and the first crocuses. See the willows
by the river start to green. Wonder how
I will shake the taste of winter and all
the sighs of family and friends.

3/19/13
6:56 PM
Stafford, VA

DEMENTIA

Thoughts clutter, footprints circle,
ideas glimmer from beneath half-read news.
My understanding deadened by others'
concerns about my well-being. Love comes
in another disguise and a flutter of hands.

The light diffused, a pale gray disc,
my moon hides behind clouds and I
am afraid to sail, sure death lies on
a reef waiting for me to rip my hull asunder.

Experience too often distorts the present.
Knowledge prevents me from seeing
what has changed and how ignorant I am
of all the newest wonders children are sure
are all that is important to existence.

Leaves flutter past me like tears in a rain.
I know seasons are changing. I wait
for the new day to burn off the Fog.
Allow me to see what it is coming
before it no longer matters.

1134
04-29-17
Stafford, VA

BIBLIOGRAPHY

Half Finished published in Prism 42
Sunday Morning Waffles " " These Human Shores Book 1 2013
Sanguine & Sagacious " " Prism 41
The End of Concordance " " Prism 41
Reflections In An Antique Mirror " " Prism 27
Tweener " " Prism Calendar for 2017
Cause There Is Poetry " " Prism 28
Take the Pot Down, Please " :" Prism 27
Crewel Points " " Prism 28
Hylas " " Prism 28
A Rake " " Prism 25
Love Never Dies " " Prism 28
Raising Sand Dollars " " Prism 14
Can You Hear The Ice Cry Against Spring's Arrival? " " Prism 29
Cranes & Kites " " Prism
Grammar " " Prism
A Beach Comber's Lament " " Prism 40

Winners of the Dr. Bruce Dawe, AO, Patronal Prize

This is a Prize given out by Prism Magazine for the best poem in that months magazine. It is chosen by a group of Professors from various English Dept. at Australian Universities from the poems in a particular month's issue. This is as I understand it. Any mistakes about what the prize represents are on my part. The winners in this book are:

A Beach Comber's Lament
On Reading
Can You Hear The Ice Cry Against Spring's Arrival
Everything published by Prism is available on Lulu

Note: I have been published in anthologies and little magazines in my life time that I did not track. Why? Because of my own anxiety and the sense it created of my not being important enough to matter, I did not keep track. Overcoming high anxiety, my life was one panic attack, was a learning process — I am still learning. I know now, I matter and this book matters. My history helped me get here, it does not define who I am or limit where I am going.

Printed in the United States
by Baker & Taylor Publisher Services